# Verses

## a book of love poetry

by

**Cleavon J. Blair**

ISBN: 1-4033-2504-9 (e-book)
ISBN: 1-4033-2505-7 (Paperback)

This book is printed on acid free paper.

1stBooks – rev. 6/4/02

*i'd like to dedicate this book to all the artists and people who have inspired
me over the course of my life.
people like miles davis, john coltrane, pat metheny, pablo neruda (the
world's greatest poet), diego rivera, ricki lee jones ('the last chance
texaco', 'company' and 'coolsville' changed my life)*

*ani difranco—
(where in the world did you come from, your music just kicks me in the
teeth…it's so good that whenever i listen to it, i just hold my hand over my
mouth and pause with shock…you truly are a musical genius),*

*the entire okayplayer.com family (?uestlove…great site, bro),
nikki giovanni,
joshua redman, a tribe called quest, de la soul, mos def, sade,
sweetback, stuart mathewman, digable planets (where y'all at),
thelonious monk, sonia sanchez, sonny fortune, bob dylan (God bless
you), pharoah sanders,
meshell ndegeocello, fiona apple,
sting, joni mitchell, jaco pastorious, julian joseph, ursula rucker, daniel
gray—kontar,
robert deniro, lyle mays, branford marsalis, spike lee,
michael wright, samuel l. jackson, dj shadow, the roots, bahamadia
alpha (your music is incredible…),
michael ondaatje('anil's ghost' and 'the english patient' are pure beauty)
madonna, wallace roney,
chris rock (you truly made me afraid of 'the tossed salad man')
michael jordan, charles barkley, larry bird,
magic Johnson,
and miss oprah winfrey…
(go'n oprah, you know you bad…)*

*amy ellen mattingly, j. renae postlethwait,
alisa marie nazelli, carisa lee lindsay, jessi hicks, julie cook,
anna deery, truli powell—borgner,
bowling green state university and the ohio state university*

*my greatest friends:
deanna donna vatan (you are the coolest woman on the planet) and
martin callahan (you're the brother i never had, love you bro!!!)*

*mathwon, can't wait to see you, bro*

*lorraine, ledeithra: what would i do without you two.  thanks for always keeping my ego in check, and being more than friends to me.  i love you both…*

*new covenant believers church in columbus, oh,
michelle vermillion,*

*amy marie henry
(i miss you wheezie),
dawn 'shamalammalammalam' thompson—love you, dude!!!*

*columbus, oh (the greatest city in the united states)*

*my family: mom (clarice diane sanders) and pop (charles a. blair, jr.)
my sister lanja, my nephew ian, my niece haley
what would i do without my family
life constantly shows me that you are the only people in this world who truly care about me
no matter what happens to me: if i go broke, if i lose my job, whatever…
you never love me any less
you just hug me and let me know that everything will be ok
you always treat me like a son, like a brother, and like an uncle
you don't know how much that means to me
i love you so much…so much that i cannot put it into words
we've all been through a lot, but whatever happens, it has never broken the bond that we have with each other.
we are so blessed…*

*and to jill kristine—the love of my life…the word love cannot describe how i feel about you…
you truly are the most remarkable woman i've ever met
your kisses are the wine my heart has desired all its life
i love you so much
and i'm so humbled and thankful that i'm the one for you
God has blessed me so much…
i hope i make your heart sing as much as you make mine dance with joy
i never really knew love until i met you
I LOVE YOU!!!!!!!!!!*

# CONTENTS

i hope you enjoy the book…
it's not perfect and has its faults, but it is still a very important
work…for me…

God Bless You…
cjb

become one

i want to make love to you
i want to kiss every part of you…
i want to love you with my hands…
i want to love you with my eyes…
i want to love you with my mouth…
i want to love you with my heart…
there is no one else…
there could never be anyone else…
my heart was exclusively made for you…
do you know that…
my body is incapable of making love to another person…
you are my twin…
you are my love…
you are my heart…
i want to feel you underneath me…
i want to feel you on top of me…
receiving my love….
slower…deeper…faster…forever…
my breath has become sweet from the sweat of your love…
i want to see your eyes…as we're loving each other…
     i want to see the kisses…that they have for me…
i want to hear your voice…as we're loving each other…
     i want to hear the kisses…that it has for me…
i want to feel your hands…touching every part of me…
feeling every part of me…that loves you…
i want to feel your hair on my face…sweaty and sweet…from the love we've made…
i want to become one with you…
merge…so to speak…
i want to be as close as humanly possible with you…
i want to feel you from the inside…
          …feel what your heart feels…
          …taste what your heart feels …
i want to feel your breath behind my ears…
          …hear the soft grunts of your love…
          …letting me know that i've pleased you…
i want to feel those strong…wet…passionate kisses in the middle of our lovemaking…
that signal our last viable way of expressing our love and need for each other…
i want to make love to you…today…
i want to make love to you…tomorrow…
i want to make love to you…yesterday…
i want to make love to you…forever…
i want the love we make to be an extension of the love we have…
i want to be consumed by you…on fire with your love…
i need to be loved by you…blanketed in your kisses

you…the one i haven't seen…you are the one…
the one who has spoken to me in my dreams on many a night…
whispering tales of love and laughter in my ears…
bringing forth a beautiful smile to my face…
my heart was halved…
…and shared with you…
my soul was halved…
…and shared with you…
how do i continue to walk on…when i know that you exist in this world for me…and i for you…
how do i continue to walk on…without you…
we are one…
how do i continue on…without part of myself…
i shall stop my progression for you…so that we may progress together…into beauty…together…
as one…one entity…our hearts sewn together…by the love we make….
i love you…for all of our days…
i love you…with all the kisses the world has to offer…
i love you…with every child's laughter…
i love you…with a love provided by God…
i love you…i love you…i love you…
my sweet soul bride…i love you…

the ring around my heart is for you…

love in2 U

your lips are always with me…
admirers observe me…
insatiably salivating to walk in the same light as me
because they feel i am the one who shouldn't be walking alone
what they don't understand is that i never walk alone…never…

they don't see the flower of your soul that climbs daily through your lips to pierce
my heart with your love…

they don't see the kisses that reside upon my face…my neck…my lips…my
heart…which mark the territory of your love…

they don't see your arm wrapped around my waist…or your hand in mine…or your
legs wrapped around mine…or our tongues locked in some sort of knot from our
kiss…or the beauty in your eyes and the love and admiration of you in mine…or my
lips dancing across the back of your neck…or my hands sailing the beautiful ocean
of your hair…

they don't see the love we've just made…

they don't see that i am your love…
they don't see that you are my love…
that's fine…
i will love you in more than just beauty…
i'll love you in the light…
i'll love you in darkness…
i'll love you in life…
i'll love you beyond life…
…my eyes…
…my hands…
…my lips…
…my tears…
…my body…
…my heart…
will love you in all God has to offer…
can i love you?
may i love you?
let's love…4ever…
let's build a love and more than a love for each other…
own me…let me be your slave…let your heart be the master of me…
i love you…now…as i have 4ever

step closer to me…
put your hands upon me and look into my eyes…share your soulful love with me…
kiss my lips…bite my lips…make me love you more than is humanly possible…
make love to me…more than is humanly possible…

i want to feel my orgasm come from my soul…
            (make me come…)
kiss my love…as i kiss yours…

make my heart scream out for you…
make my heart scream out for you…
make my heart scream out for you…
yeah…make me scream for you…

kiss the beauty back into my life…
love your beauty into my life…
while i love love into yours….

love

my words come from my heart…
it…my heart…speaks as though it were my own mouth…
what does it speak of…
is speaks of you…it speaks of the music that your being sends flying through my soul…
it speaks of the beauty of your words and the softness of your kiss…
and it is this kiss…that reminds me that i am loved…by you… and by God…
your kiss is not a physical kiss…but a spiritual one…
it wraps its arms around my waist…it stares into my eyes…it kisses the nape of my neck…and it smiles at my heart…
with a joy derived from pure recognition of our two hearts rushing together…
in a world of confusion…to find a balance that we two can only provide for each other…
you love me…
you love me…
you love me…
with your laughter…
you love me…
with your words…
you love me…
with the beauty of your soul…
i walk through the valley of death…looking for one ray of light…
one shred of hope…
and through the darkness…i trudge…i trudge…
slapping away the darkness of the demons which try to attach themselves to me…
my strength grows…and grows…until it weakens me…and it's this hope…your light…that i need to survive in this world…
i understand that i need it…this ray of light…
to complete my journey through this version of hell…
and when i think i will not find it…
i look miles ahead of me…over the smoke…over the flames…over the putrid stench of this world…
and i see you…with not a flag in hand…but a light…which i recognize as your heart…
…clothed in words..
and i run…i run to your words…for they don't want to take anything from me…
they want to give me love…
and kisses on warm sunday mornings…
your words want nothing more than to rub against my words in the middle of the night…
your words want to kiss me with honesty…with truth…with love…
and i…after feeling the strength and beauty and love of your words…
will oblige in being all that you need…
it is now our world…
a world which is now filled with the warmth of the sun's rays…
a world that is filled with laughter…

a world God would be proud of…
and in this world…we walk…through the rain…
with the big…fat…beautiful…raindrops…tickling the tops of our foreheads…
tickling our tongues…as we stick them out…to taste the freshness of the rain…
i'll take you on a journey where we put on paper pirate hats…
and walk through the jungles of our hearts…
squishing mud between the toes of our beautiful feet…
and at the end of the day…we'll sit down…smile at each other…kiss each other…love each other…
and eat peanut butter and jelly sandwiches for dinner…
can you see this?  can you feel this?
i can now see myself quoting the words of me'shell ndegeocello into your ear…
"such pretty hair…may i kiss you…may i kiss you there…so beautiful…so beautiful…you are…"
and then i'd take you in my arms…
and together…we'd drift…
…drift off…
to a wonderful sleep…

for my love

my sweet love
i am so glad that you waited for me
i am so glad that i waited for you
can you imagine your heart if we hadn't met
i truly think my life would be over
the number of steps in my life began to decrease
until you kissed my heart
i too have been ogled in hunger
but love i knew something new and right had to be awaiting my presence
as i awaited the presence of another
then you kissed me
you kissed me and you didn't even know it
i didn't even know it
you kissed me long
you kissed me hard
you kissed me passionately
you kissed me lovingly
you kissed me slow
you kissed me with your heart
you kissed me with your mind
you kissed me with your soul
and believe it or not
you kissed me with your body
your kisses are strong and plentiful
i am still dazed and dazzled by your beauty
as i will be for the rest of our lives
you are everything to me
you are the sun in my heart
you are the seed in my heart
you are the beautiful rain in my heart
you plant yourself in my soil
nurture yourself with your beautiful rain in my heart
and you grew there like the beautiful lily that you are
you have grown to become my heart
i love you
those words do not describe what you mean to me
the words escape my lips
but the feeling fills my heart
i have a dream where we stand in each other's arms
and our hearts are touching each others
and there we communicate our love to each other
on some level where our minds have not the capacity to understand
we just love
i want to kiss you so bad right now
i want you to see the tears of joy flowing through me
you are my wife

you have been all of my life
whispering in my ears in those years when i was just a little boy
not knowing who you were, but understanding the pure joy and love
of your presence and your words
you've kissed me my whole life
brought me so much joy
so much companionship
so much love
i only hope i do it for you
i love you honey…

honeybabysweetiesugar

honey
kiss me
i'm dying
i'm dying to devour the sweet delicious fires of your…
…mouth…
my lips are now wet with your kisses
my lips are now wet with you
my palate will never be cleansed of its taste for you

i am for you

i have this image of you now…
an image of you lying in my arms…
the coolness and softness of the grass all around us…
i look into your eyes…
and smile at the recognition of our hearts…
i'm loving you with my eyes…
i'm loving you with my heart…
i'm loving you with the soft touch of my hand…
and you…are loving me with that scent of yours…
the beautiful scent of your hair…
it's fragrance tickling my soul as one tickles a child…
your hair is gently blowing in my face…
you are giving me hair kisses…
suddenly…you stop smiling…and you stare at me intently…seriously…
and your eyes speak to me…
they say… "please kiss me…please love me…"
my heart responds with no words…only action…
my heart tells my hand to feel the beauty of your hair…
to soak up the love in your eyes…like a sponge…
and then my heart tells me to…kiss you….
i see your internal tears…and feel mine as well…as we kiss…
we have truly found a piece of heaven…in this world…between you and i…
you are the love of my life…
you always have been…and now my heart only begins to remember the days…
of long ago…of your finger…tracing my lips…
preparing my lips for the love of your mouth and your heart…
darling…i am killed…by your beauty…
since i know that i must die…i want to die knowing your love…
i want to die living in your love…
i want to die dancing in your love…
i want to die loving in your love…
i want to kiss my entire being into your heart…
so that you may feel the amount of love that i have for you…
i want to skip through the park…through life…with your beauty…
at my side…
i want my love and strength to be near you always…protecting you…shielding
you…
from the ills of this world…
i want you to know of only the beautiful things…
so many beautiful things are hidden…but i see them…and i want to reveal them to
you…
i want to carve a world for you and i…a place where we can thrive…be happy…
look at each others feet…
and tell each other corny jokes…which constantly remind us that we are here for
each other…
you are my sunshine…

upon hearing your heart…the clouds seemed to be pushed away…by you…
by your smile…
by your heart…
by the beautiful glow of your eyes…
kiss me…i beg of you…kiss me
kiss me hard…
kiss me slow…
kiss me the way only you can kiss me…
honey…my soul is starved…for you…
kiss me…and feed me with the beauty of your heart…
the sustenance of your love strengthens me…which allows me to love you like you need…
i can be your heart…
i can be your soul…
i can be your love…
i am your heart…
i am your soul…
i am your love…
and this love…will always be with you…it shall never cease in its longing for you…
it will be the beautifully sweet flame that dances forever between us…
nothing will shake the stoicism of our shared love…
God ordained it that way…
the tears slowly flow down my cheeks…in reverence…thankfulness…
for this gift of you…
i too "wish and pray…
hoping my desperation…will make you as real and lovely as i have imagined you to be…"
honey…i am real…i am love…your love…
i am your kiss…
i am your hand…
i am your eyes…
i am your lips…
i am your hair…
i am your love…
i am you…
to know my reality…look in your mirror…
and whisper my name…
and you will find yourself immersed in the pool of love that is my heart…your heart…our heart
i am loving you always…
kissing you…always…
smiling with you…at you…always…
i am right by your side…always…
as you are with me…

i love your language…
i love your words…
i love your love…
i love you…

my love

your love
that's what i am
your love

a love seen only by you
a love felt only by you
a love made for only you

you
you are my love
i write for only you
and my writing
it isn't lonely anymore
it is so happy and comforted by you
by your words
by the beauty of your mind
by the beauty of your soul
by the beauty of you
i love you

can you feel my kisses
they are running towards you at a million miles an hour
colliding with the beauty of your lips

can you feel my mind
it is loving you through the space that exists between us

can you feel my fingers
tickling you all over like the bubbles of your bubble bath

can you feel my heart
making love to you with the beautiful passion of syrup
slowly moving across every bit of you
sharing my sweetness with you
welding us together with its stickiness

i feel your kisses
running racing to meet mine with an intensity and love
previously foreign to me

i feel your mind
smiling and loving me with the beautiful smile of your eyes

i feel your fingers
i feel your hands
on my face

on my back
on me
massaging the love and peace and promise back into my heart

i feel your heart
matching the love our bodies share
matching the love our souls share
i feel the warmth of the closeness of you

my love
that's what you are
my love

love you in beauty

there is no substitute for you
nothing can replace what your heart has given mine
i remember walking through the door of your heart
…unannounced…and probably unwanted…
all i knew is that i was hurt and bleeding…
…and you were too…
i could feel the magic in the beautiful kisses you'd planted upon a stranger…
those kisses were a language…
no different than english…japanese…spanish…but altogether more…
you spoke our language…
a language of truth…
a language of desire…
a language of passion…
a language of love…
and this language…it isn't spoken verbally…through one's mouth…
this language isn't even heard through one's ears…
it is seen…it is felt…
by every being of your body…worn…if you will…like a shirt…
it is this love that i felt…in you…and…in me…
and honey…you finally opened your door completely
and shared your soul with me…you loved me…
loved me back into a glorious beauty…where the face of you…
was all the sunshine i'd ever need…
i want to love you…
take you on a magical ride…
through the beautiful hills of tuscany…
reveling in the beauty of the green of san gimignano…
drinking the heart of the villages in the deep reds of the glasses of pungent
chiantis…
i want to travel the world with you…
experience all of the world's beauty…with the world's most beautiful woman…
loving you in beauty…that is what i dream of…loving you…forever in beauty…
i'd truly make you my bride…my bride…in happiness…
my bride…in beauty…
my bride…in love

murderer...

i was shot today…
i thought i would die…
suffocate in the blood of my passion…
derived from the beautiful ramblings of your heart…
shoot me again…or…stab me…i dare you
pierce me with the beauty of your heart…
impale me with the beauty of your words…
beat me with your heart…
strangle me with the loveliness of you…
drown me with your affection…
murder me with your heart…
murder me with your lips…
murder me with your body…
murder me with your love…
but first…
love me with the tenderness of your kiss…
…love me…
with the tenderness of you…

my love II

you will never meet another like me...
as i will never meet another like you...
my love is unique...

its touch defines the word gentle
its touch defines the word beautiful
its touch defines the word love

its kiss...
        ...is as relaxing as a fine glass of wine...
        ...and as electric as a lightening storm...
            (it will shock you with its lips)
its taste...
        ...is as sweet as peach and blueberry cobbler on a breezy fall day...
        ...as divine as raspberry sorbet cheesecake on a hot summer day...

my love is unique...
...beautiful as no other...

my love is the rain
my love is the sun
my love is a baby's smile
my love...
        ...well...
my love...is you...

you are my love...
you are the smile in my eyes...
you are the passion in my touch...
you are the breeziness in my heart...
you...are me...as...i am you...

let our kiss become one of magic...
one of peace...
one of love...
one of wonder...

let the circle of our arms...our embrace...be known as home...to you and i

let the love of our eyes shine brightly upon us
        ...and upon the world...
        ...reminding the world...
that true love is indeed possible...

i love you more than my words can say...
i love you more than my touch can say...

i love you more than my eyes can say…
i love you more than my heart can say…
i love you more than i can say…
my love…my beautiful love…
…you are the most beautiful being my soul has ever encountered…
God must be smiling upon me…for my love for you is limitless…
and my dreams are filled with your kisses

shared poetry

when i hear your voice
… in word…
it reminds me of my favorite poet…
…the great pablo neruda…
his muse tapped him on the shoulder as a child…
it (his muse) touched me…as has yours…
your muse…your mind…your spirit…
i can feel them…
i can hear them…
reverberating in the halls of my being…

your voice is a sound that i desperately long to hear…

you see, my world is quite a beautiful world…
but outside my world…which is all around me…
…no one speaks from their heart…
…no one speaks from their spirit…
…no one speaks from their own muse…
…to hear the strength of the passion in your heart turns my belly to jelly…
…my soul smiles internally and externally…
i don't know you, but i know your words…
i know your voice… they have spoken to me my entire life…
spoken to me on those rainy days when your muse overwhelmed you…
i am here…many miles away… hearing that voice… on some level unbeknownst to
me…
it creeps in…whispering my name… begging me to listen…
i've tried not to listen… but if i don't listen then i implode…
and i too do not want crap on me…
so i stretch out my ears…my soul…
…to the sounds of your words…
…to the sounds of your voice…
…to the sounds of your muse…
and i listen…
and i enjoy…
and i love…
and i live…
in the beauty that is you…
it leads me to fly…
above all of which that is known to my eyes, but not my soul…
i soar…like the eagle that i am…
with your sound…your voice…your words…your muse… coursing my veins…
like the life blood that sustains me…
it is the light in my darkness…
the triumphant flag waving through all of the chaos…
my hope is… that one day…you will be real…and true…
so, on those rainy days… know that i sit…

sit in front of the window… glass of wine in hand…
and i listen…
i listen for your truth…
i listen for your sound…
…beckoning like a siren to come and fly away…
i live…to be silent in your silence…
or be the sound of the words that emanate from you…
smile…
smile knowing that i smile…
…whenever you send me your presence…

the sound of your voice

yes…
…bless me with your voice…
it drips…like a slow thick honey…
over my ears…
over my face…
over my…….lips….

mmmmm…your voice is so sweet…

it brings to mind the beautifully strong and peaceful passion of miles davis…
the sexiness of the trumpet…slowing massaging the notes into my heart…into my
soul…
i would love to…kiss your voice…
kiss it…and stare into its eyes…
to let it know how much i appreciate it…
to let it know how much it does for me…
to let it know how much i long for it…
to let it know how much i need it…

mmmmm…your voice is so sweet…

without it…i'm nothing more than a diabetic…
a diabetic whose blood sugar level has dipped too low…
in need of no orange juice…
in need of no candy…
in need of only you…
talk to me…
say my name…
mouth the sugar back into my soul…
slow kiss the energy of your heart into mine…

and with this kiss…
        give me…
your voice…
        give me…
your smile…
        give me…
your touch…
        give me…
your smell…
        give me…
your heart…
        give me…
your love…
        give me…
you…

i love you...

50

warm together

will you give me your love
for i have given you mine
give me that sweet kiss of yours…
        …the strength of it
        …the sex of it
        …the sharpness of it
        …the wetness of it
        …the love of it
        …the you of it
i want to be yours
i want you to be mine
i imagine us kissing
kissing so much that our lips become numb and weakened with each kiss
i imagine us making love
so much love
that our bodies become sore with the amount of love we give each other
i see us sitting in a crowd of our peers
together
you and i
and the secret of the depth of our love belongs to only us
the smiles of giddiness in our hearts
are reminders of our shared memories of intimacies of the hours before
honey
you have saved my life
i was dying
eternal life was on the trail of my heart
the beauty in my heart was ignored by all that the world has to offer
i had given up on the 'special' part of me
i was ready to travel the road of everyone else
but you…
        …your words came out of nowhere
        …your heart delicately stroked the tendrils of my hair
        …and made sweet sweet love to my body
God stepped in and saved me from the path of the masses
he brought me to you…
and you to me
images of your eyes pass through my mind often
i see the light they exude when you smile and when you love
you
are my soul mate
and you arrived at a time
when my belief in true love was fading
you are with me yet you are not with me
i wish your face…your heart…your eyes…your lips…your love…
were the first and last things i see everyday
i want to wake with you

live with you
love with you
kiss with you
and then at night sleep with you
i want to feel your body close to mine
in the comfort of my arms
where the light strands of your hair tickle my face as we drift into sleep
and the aroma of you permeates through all of my senses
oh how warm we would be together
no matter the temperature of the world
in our hearts…in our home…in our bed…
we…would be warm…together…

sometimes i need you...

sometimes i need you...

when the sunshine no longer brings a smile to my face
when the smiles of faces no longer seem true
and the world seems a tad bit...off center
my heart...
my soul...
my being...
all carry me to you...
your smile...it always reminds me of who i really am...
a man who has a need to bath in peace...and the artist's beauty in the world...
a man who needs love...
a man who needs you...

in order to find happiness...
in order to find peace...
in order to find love...
i again must step away from the world...
and run back to the beauty of your heart...
if you'll have me...

no one's come near...since we last loved...
no one's tasted the wine of my lips and the wind of my hips
no one's felt the passion of my touch...and the beauty of my gaze
no one's felt the breeze of my heart or heard the rhythmic sound of my voice
...because sometimes i need you...
honey...i've got it bad and there surely ain't no cure...
make me smile again...

make love…

in my mind…it starts this way…
        …you look at me…
        …you kiss me with your eyes…
        …you kiss me with your beautifully strong hands…
        …you kiss my gleaming bald head…with those never ending lips of
yours…
i scream a thousand words to you through my kisses…

my lips want everything…they want it all
my lips want to caress your feet…
my lips want the taste of your legs…
my lips want to feel the sensitivity of your inner thighs…
my lips want to tease you by softly…
        they want to tease you…gently…
        they want to tease you…purposely…
my lips want to slightly rub…
        …then pass over your…poo poo la la…
        …saving it for later…
my lips want to sail the nape of your neck…
        …letting you feel…slightly…the rough edges of my teeth…
your cheeks…eyes…ears…hands…need to be introduced to the softness of my
lips…
my lips need to know…visit…every curve…every line…of your body…
my lip kisses then turn into deep seductive hand kisses…
        …which start at the very top of your beautiful body…
        …running their fingers through the soft strands of silk…otherwise known
as your hair…
tracing and making a path down the back of your neck to that magnificent island of
yours…
        …also known as the great back of renae…
        …so wide…yet so petite and feminine…
which in turn leads to one of the seven wonders of my world…
        …renae's ass!
an ass…butt, if you will…
that is sheer perfection…
holding mystery…as if it were nothing more than a fragile newborn baby…
it doesn't seem to be there…it hides…waiting for the touch of my hands…
to bring it forth into the light…
a kiss then…from my lips…on the eastern cheek….then the western cheek…
is enough to shake the stoicism of my soul…
that's ok…i'd gladly give her…and her bright body…enough of my strength…to
last a lifetime…

my sweet renae…
        …kiss me with your hands…
        …kiss me with your eyes…

your music is so very beautiful…
             …it seems to crawl under my skin…
and my cup of coffee…with your cream added…
seems to rush over when thoughts of you pop into my head…
these thoughts rush in naturally…as if they were supposed to be there…
for me and for you…

kiss me with your love
             …for your love pushes…
it pushes me to the point where i want to kiss you…
i want to kiss you…where all life begins…
i want to kiss your beauty…treasure it…like a gift from God…
i want to make love…
i need to make love…
             …make love to your mind sweetheart…
             …as i'm so attracted to it…
i just want to kiss it…to let it know…what my core is all about…
i want to bathe your soul in my sunshine…
can we do that…
             …can i kiss your soul…
             …can i kiss your mind…
             …can i kiss your heart…
may i hear your music…
may i kiss your music…
play your music…for me…
             …play for me…
             …play for me…
please…
             …play for me!…
i'm ready…
i'm ready to listen…to your heart…
and to make love…
             …ready to make love to your soul…
             …ready to make love to your mind!…

so what

yeah…i loved you…but so what…
that is how cynical i've become…
to the one thing that defines me so…

love isn't meant for me…
i'm just an observer of it…studying it…like a scientist would study a reaction of
various chemicals thrown together for…scientific purposes…

what is my function…why am i here…is there a purpose for this feeling…
            why am i one who can see love dancing in the air…
kissing the lips and hearts of people who don't completely understand what it is and
what it is all about
            but why is love not reserved for me…
my eyes see…but my heart isn't allowed to dance so lovingly and rhythmically as
the others…

i always thought i'd walk my path in this world alone…hoping…praying that i
might have the opportunity…just once
            …to wake with love lying by my side…
            to live and love God's beauty…with love…
            to have love depend on my heart…to depend on my love…
but what i get…is…
"yes…you loved me…like no other…and made me see a beautiful light in the world
that i'd never seen before…but so what…" (it doesn't matter…….)

is life worth a thousand deaths of the heart…
is the inspiration and sight of love…worth the time…
must i keep walking…
when parking is all i want to do…
why have a gift that you cannot experience…
take it away…make me forget it…blind me to the beauty that is shared by those all
around me…for it does nothing but steal life from my heart…life that can no longer
be restored by anyone's magic…it is dying a slow…painful…inconsequential
death…
no longer do i want to press the pause button of my love…of my heart…i want to
remove the music completely…and turn the system off…as love means nothing…to
me…

a new love

the sun has set…and our love and life together…are no more…
they have been over for sometime now…
i now realize that i'll never hear the music of your voice again…
nor will i ever see the peace exuding from your beautifully strong strut…
or the passionate gaze of your eyes…
those are all things of the past…memories of a time long ago…a much simpler time…
when our love was all that we needed…
i wish you could see me now…
basking in the beautiful…peaceful…sun of arizona…

living…
without a smile on my face…

(for you took it with you…when you left)

living…
with a wonderful strength which is teetering on the edge of weakness…

(because you also took that with you)

you stole my gift…
you stole my love…
you stole my heart…
like a thief in the night…or better yet…like a cheap con man…
and sold them at a corner pawn shop for $25.11…
you sold them and used them to bargain for a love…not really considered love…
you bought a love…from a man…who believes in submission…your submission…in all that you do…
(it's so sad)
now i see that it's probably for the better…
i realize that all people don't feel the need to fly above the ugliness of the world…
forever in love…forever in freedom…forever in peace…
so i soar alone…
and when i fly down to see old friends…i'll pass your abode…
i promise to stop and say hello…
but…
if i see…your eyes yearning for the freedom and love you decided to give up…
i will remind you that YOU chose death with him over life with ME…
and i'll just fly away…with my memory of you…
forever coursing the veins of my heart…until…
i find a new love…

suma

my love…
i think i have found you…
God willing…i have found you…
i've waited my whole life for this moment…

the moment when i first stare into your beautiful eyes…
the moment when their beauty caress my heart…
in a way that only you can…

your eyes…your soul…your heart…
have kissed me so beautifully…
…you and i…
we understand nothing…except Love…
that is the gift that God gave the both of us…
no other can have me…save for you…
i've been lonely every minute of my life…save for the moments that i'm with
you…
i will walk slowly…truthfully…and honestly…
for you…with you…
do not be afraid to open your heart to me…
i have nothing for you except the beauty that God has given me…
it's all i have…and honey…i give it all to you…

just please…listen…trust the voice of God…
…as He tells you our story…
except for God…we are all we have in this world…
love me so that i may love you…
i want to swim in the rivers of your heart…
…swim in the rivers of your love…
i need you…in order to keep walking…to keep living…to keep loving…
i am dead without you…
i am nothing except a piece of living nothingness…without you…
honor our love…honor God's love…
bless me with your continued presence…at night…in our bed…
side by side…and together we will begin a new day…
we will brave the ugliness of the world…only to have the blessing of God…
who will let us run from the ugliness…into the beauty of our own love…
it's you…that I need…
i want to feel your hair…napping on the strength of my shoulder…
your hair…loving me with your beauty…
i need your hands close to me…
letting my body know your need for me…
i love you honey…
i've waited a lifetime for your smile…make us happy…
bring the smile back to my heart…
bring your kisses to me…and i will turn them into tears…

beautiful tears of happiness…beautiful tears of our love…
i will love you like no other…
there isn't a man in this world capable of loving you the way i can…
God made it so…
so honey…take my hand…
walk with me into the beautiful place that God has created for us…
love me now…love me tomorrow…love me forever…
and my kisses…my love…
will blanket you for all eternity…
we have something true…(LOVE)
…and this LOVE…is DIVINE…
you just have to trust God's words…
…trust HIM…
for He will lead us to beauty…
    He will lead us to happiness…
    He will lead us to love…

your absence

honey, i do not want your absence tonight
i need you here…at my side…
you see…at this moment…my heart and my soul aren't quite strong enough to stand
on their own…
it is you that i need at this moment…
it is the strength of your beautiful kisses that i need…
my knees are all wobbly, and i cannot stand much longer…
honey…the man in me is almost gone…
it is slowly being withered away by time…
being withered away by loneliness…
being withered away by a lovelessness that seems to be the only constant in my
life…
i am sinking…
…slowly, but very surely…
and all i need for survival is for you to sing me to sleep…each and every night…
i don't know who you are…
i don't know where you are…
but i know you're here somewhere…
…walking…waiting…
to meet the purity of my gaze…
to kiss the love into my heart…
honey…
you must hurry because i'm very near the end of my rope…
where my heart will wither and die…
turn into a pile of dust…where it will settle for a heart not destined for me…
where it will settle into a life of unhappiness…
because it thirsts for love…doing anything for it…no matter the shame…
so honey…please understand…
i do not want your absence tonight…
i need you here…right by my side…
living…
loving…
kissing…
fucking…for love…

julie

nearly five years have passed…
and still you reside in my heart…
you have made my heart your home…
you have made my heart your life…
you have made my heart your heart…

you've taken ownership of all that i am,
but you leave me on the shore of your heart…
waiting for your return…which i know will never come…

don't sing to me…you siren of the deep
don't dance through the recesses of my mind…your steps are too rhythmical for my
offbeat steps…
don't stare into my eyes…the brightness of your eyes blinds me…
don't touch me…for my skin is much too sensitive for your touch…
don't kiss me…for my lips are much too chapped to bear the beauty of yours…
don't love me…for my heart has not the strength to endure your kind of love…

you've taken more than my heart…
          for my smile is also missing…
you've taken more than my smile…
          for my passion is also missing…
you've taken more than my passion…
          for my love is also missing…

nothing makes much sense to me anymore…
because i only know half of what i see…
for i'm not whole without you…

you've taken a part of me…and kept it for yourself…
i cannot function without it…i cannot function without you…
you have wounded my soul, sweetheart…
and there is nothing to heal it…save for a miracle from God…

my lips are destined to be numbed for the rest of my days…
i have seen the mountaintops of love…
…and without you…
i must now wade in the valley of 'nothingness'
alone…and never drink from the flask of love again…

love is my essence…and it has been stolen from me…
my essence is gone…and without it…what am i…
merely one of the walking dead…a zombie…
feeling nothing more than the contempt others have for me…

Lord…

could there possibly be…
any miracles left for me…

my wait for jill kristine

i am a man now…
no longer taken with the beauty of girls…

my heart has run into the heart of a woman…
a woman who has shown me the beauty of being a man…

she has given me the courage to kiss her…
she has given me the courage to live with her…
she has given me the courage to love her…
and most importantly…
she has given me the courage to be her husband…

to take her hand…
and walk our paths through life
        …meeting every challenge
        …jumping over every obstacle…
                        kissing…
                loving…
        laughing…
TOGETHER…
this love…
is the blessing from God that every man should pray for…
love is truly beautiful…when you wait for the one destined for you…

give it to you

i live and love
like a man
when i'm about to kiss her lips
…i stare into her eyes
…to let her know that i love her
…and that i'm not afraid to love her

when i kiss her lips
…i kiss my heart into her entire being

i want her to feel my love for her through my kiss…
i want her to feel my sex for her through my kiss…

i want my lips to move across hers…
        strong…and wet…
not playful…but with a surety of what they want to share with her…

i want to love her with my hands
i want to love her with my eyes
i want to love her with my mouth

and my manhood…wants to love her with itself…

please her…
        as she's never been pleased before
for in that pleasure…lies my love…

as strong as my sex…
as strong as the muscles she feels in my back
as strong as the muscles she feels in my arms…
as powerful as the thrusts of my pelvis
will my love be for her…
unyielding until her passionate screams beg me to relent…
she will be pleased in all aspects of my love…
        her body will be pleased…
        and most importantly…her heart will be pleased…
leaving no doubt…that i am the man for her…

my kisses…
will wash away all the kisses of those that came before me…

my touch…
will remove the fingerprints of those that came before me…

my sex…
will remove any memory of those before me…

she will be mine…and i will be hers…

the sun shines upon me

finally…
the rain has stopped…
the beating of the large cold drops has ceased …
for the time being…
the sun has decided that it wants to shine upon me …
it wants to kiss my lips…
it wants to kiss my cheeks…
it wants to hold my hand…
…and make love to my body….

so beautiful this sunshine is….
i feel as if i'm floating…
better yet…walking…walking on a cloud of beauty….
all now seems possible…
all now seems probable…
all now feels like love…

bright and positive…
strong and melodic…like the sounds of coltrane's horn…
the sun's rays pick me up …
and take me on a journey of happiness…
could it be that i have died…and gone to heaven…
or could it be that i'm in love…

my kisses now have meaning…
my touch now has emotion…
and my eyes now show tenderness…
i feel human now…
like i fit in someone's world…
true love can be so empowering…
it makes you strong and brave enough
to be the kid your heart so desires to be…and the man that it has to be…

thank you God…
for spinning the handle of my blinds in the opposite direction…
and allowing this beautiful light to shine upon me…
You have given me purpose…
You have given me life…
You have given me Love…

and this Love is so beautiful…
it never allows me to be unhappy…
it never allows me to turn and walk into darkness…
it forever shines brightly upon me…
and has taught me the infinite beauty of life…
every day with her is absolutely wonderful…

from the time i see her hair flying in all directions in the morning…
to the time i walk in the door in the evening…
all of this love is there…for me…
it isn't flung at me…with a desperation behind it…
it is shared with me…as mine is shared with her…

thank you for answering my prayers…

thank you for not forgetting about me…

i miss you

i remember when we first met…

i didn't want you and you didn't want me…
but you eventually showed me your heart…accidentally…
i'm still blinded by its light…

i still remember how i felt when you gave me your phone number…
i felt as if God had answered all of my prayers…
you were my angel…

i even remember how scared i was to kiss you…
i was afraid i would fall even further…

but i kissed you anyway…and i fell…hard
my heart became yours
i became yours
my love…
…it was all for you…

the sound of your voice became the only music my heart would know
i remember the kisses from your beautiful mouth
i remember how i fell in love with you each and every time you said my name
i remember how your touch shook the foundation of my soul

i remember how my heart would jump and dance at the mere sight of you

i really loved you
i thought my life…and heart…would always be with you
…but you walked away…so easily
i finally know what pain feels like…as my soul aches for you

i always pictured us kissing in our old age…
but i know that day will never come…
God has ordained it that way…

but i miss you…
not everyday…not every week…not every month…
but on calm…quiet…evenings…
your presence comes dancing back to me…
i remember you in all your splendor…all your beauty…
and my heart weeps…it sobs out loud…
…in its yearning for you…

      i miss your smile…
      i miss your eyes…
      i miss your hands…

i miss your feet...
i miss your voice...
in short...
...i miss you...

love you forever

sexy girl…

where are you tonight…

i not only need your kisses…
i not only need your smile…
          but i need your sex…

i need to feel our lips lock passionately…
          i don't want to hear your voice…
          save for the sounds of pleasure coming from you…

i want to feel your skin pressed against mine…
our bodies hot…sweating…in their longing…
to become one…

i need no lights…
just you
          touching me…

i want to look in your eyes…
          while you're on top of me
and speak to you with my eyes…
share with you how much i need to be with you
          …this way…right now

when i'm behind you…
          slightly pulling your hair…
          and loving you…the way you need it…
know that i'm crying inside…because my soul so needs this…
from you…
          this way…right now

when i'm on top you…
          and your hand caresses the muscles in my back
          while the other caresses the muscles in my butt
          and i pull up and out
          only to plunge myself deeper into you
i want to hear you moan
i want to hear your heart scream for me
          scream for my love
          scream for me to pleasure you…
i don't want to speak verbal words with you
i don't want my heart to speak to you
i want my eyes and my body to speak to you
          the way yours speak to me…

i want my mouth to speak to you
        the way yours speaks to me…

i can almost taste the pain from your lips biting mine…

i want to become drunk in the scent of your perfume…
i want to become drunk in the scent of your sex…
i want to become drunk with you…

        leave the taste of you
                on my lips…forever…
        leave the thought of you
                in my mind forever…

# About the Author

*Cleavon J. Blair is a graduate of Bowling Green State University, and currently resides in the Chicago, Illinois area.  He works as a software engineer.  You will be happy to know that he has met the love of his life, and they are engaged to be married.*